Tiny-Spiny Animals

Horned Toads

Lola M. Schaefer

Heinemann Library
Chicago, Illinois

© 2004 Heinemann Library
a division of Reed Elsevier, Inc
Chicago, Illinois

Customer Service 888-454-2279
Visit our website at www.heinemannlibrary.com

Designed by Sue Emerson, Heinemann Library; Page layout by Que-Net Media
Printed and bound in the United States by Lake Book Manufacturing, Inc.
Photo research by Scott Braut

08 07 06 05 04
10 9 8 7 6 5 4 3 2 1

Library of Congress Cataloging-in-Publication Data
Schaefer, Lola M., 1950-
  Horned toads / Lola M. Schaefer.
      v. cm. – (Tiny-spiny animals)
Contents: What are horned toads? – Where do horned toads live? – What do horned toads look like? – What do horned toads feel like? – How do horned toads use their horns? – How big are horned toads? – How do horned toads move? – What do horned toads eat? – Where do new horned toads come from?
  ISBN 1-4034-3243-0 (HC), ISBN 1-4034-3328-3 (Pbk.)
  1. Horned toads–Juvenile literature. [1. Horned toads.] I. Title.
  QL666.L267S32 2003
  597.95–dc21

                                  2003002072

Acknowledgments
The author and publishers are grateful to the following for permission to reproduce copyright material:
Title page, pp. 8, 15, 16 Karl H. Switak/Photo Researchers, Inc.; p. 4 Joe McDonald/Animals Animals; pp. 5, 6 Joe McDonald/Visuals Unlimited; p. 7 C. C. Lockwood/Animals Animals; pp. 9, 22, 24 E. R. Degginger/Animals Animals; p. 10 David Welling/Animals Animals; p. 11 Francois Gohier/Photo Researchers, Inc.; p. 12 G. C. Kelley/Photo Researchers, Inc.; pp. 13, 20 Wade Sherbrooke; p. 14 Jack Couffer/Bruce Coleman Inc.; p. 17 Larry Ditto/Bruce Coleman Inc.; p. 18 Joe DiStefano/Photo Researchers, Inc.; p. 19 R. Van Nostrand/Photo Researchers, Inc.; p. 21 Chuck Place/PlaceStockPhoto.com; p. 23 (column 1, T-B) A. N. T./NHPA, E. R. Degginger/Animals Animals, Corbis; (column 2, T-B) Joe McDonald/Animals Animals, Courtesy of High Resolution X-Ray CT Facility, University of Texas at Austin; back cover (L-R) A. N. T./NHPA, Joe McDonald/Animals Animals

Cover photograph by Karl H. Switak/Photo Researchers, Inc.

Special thanks to our advisory panel for their help in the preparation of this book:
Alice Bethke, Library Consultant
Palo Alto, CA

Eileen Day, Preschool Teacher
Chicago, IL

Kathleen Gilbert,
Second Grade Teacher
Round Rock, TX

Sandra Gilbert,
Library Media Specialist
Fiest Elementary School
Houston, TX

Jan Gobeille, Kindergarten Teacher
Garfield Elementary
Oakland, CA

Angela Leeper,
Educational Consultant
Wake Forest, NC

Some words are shown in bold, **like this.**
You can find them in the picture glossary on page 23.

Contents

What Are Horned Toads?

Horned toads are animals with bones.

They are **vertebrates**.

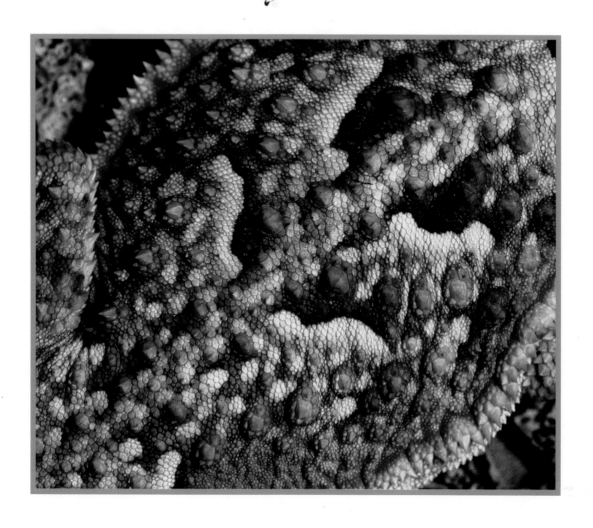

Horned toads are not toads at all.

They are really lizards, and lizards have **scales**.

Where Do Horned Toads Live?

Most horned toads live in **deserts.**

They don't need much water to live.

Horned toads make their homes
in loose soil.

They dig in **sand** and dirt.

What Do Horned Toads Look Like?

Horned toads can look like thick pancakes.

They are flat and round.

scales horns

Horned toads have **horns** on their heads.

They have **scales** on their bodies.

What Do Horned Toads Feel Like?

horns

Horned toads' heads feel bumpy.

Their **horns** are hard and sharp.

Horned toads' bodies feel bumpy, too.

Their **scales** feel like rough tree bark.

How Do Horned Toads Use Their Horns?

Horned toads use their **horns** to stay safe.

Horned toads puff up their bodies.

Then, their horns and **scales** look bigger.

Their horns scare away their enemies.

How Big Are Horned Toads?

Young horned toads are very small.

One is about as big as a finger.

Adult horned toads are a little larger.

One could fit in your hand.

How Do Horned Toads Move?

Horned toads do not hop like toads.

They walk on four legs.

Horned toads can run, too.

What Do Horned Toads Eat?

Horned toads eat ants.

They eat other bugs, too.

Horned toads sit and wait for bugs.

Then, they catch them with their sticky tongues.

Where Do New Horned Toads Come From?

Female horned toads dig holes in **sand**.

They lay many eggs in the holes.

Later, baby horned toads come out
of the eggs.

Quiz

What are these horned toad parts?

Can you find them in the book?

Look for the answers on page 24.

? ?

Picture Glossary

desert
page 6

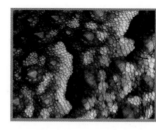
scale
pages 5, 9,
11, 13

horn
pages 9, 10,
12–13

vertebrate
(VUR-tuh-brate)
page 4

sand
pages 7, 20

Note to Parents and Teachers

Reading for information is an important part of a child's literacy development. Learning begins with a question about something. Help children think of themselves as investigators and researchers by encouraging their questions about the world around them. Each chapter in this book begins with a question. Read the question together. Look at the pictures. Talk about what you think the answer might be. Then read the text to find out if your predictions were correct. Think of other questions you could ask about the topic, and discuss where you might find the answers.

! CAUTION: Remind children that it is not a good idea to handle wild animals. Children should wash their hands with soap and water after they touch any animal.

Index

Answers to quiz on page 22

scales   horns